The Luna Erratum

a desire that is part animal, part human, part astral body. Let them transfix you.

— Nadia de Vries, author of *I Failed to Swoon* (Dostoyevsky Wannabe, 2021)

*

In Maria Sledmere's *The Luna Erratum*, rivulets of neon daylight stream through the ever-quickening fibre-optic cables of the soul. Beneath 'morphine clouds' climates change as human groans crosspollinate in the moon's tread. Sledmere concentrates the neural pathways on the world spirit, crossmatching the matters of attention. The lines grasp at what repositories of sentiment might be made secure for poetic memory, as the pleasure of every experience is threatened by its immediate disappearance, like Bernadette Mayer reciting Keats in the abandoned sea life centre. And yet, for the poet's eye, the sumptuous bounties of the world are still all up for grabs; the human squats on top of the non-human and: 'you can take bites from the sun'. This book is a hot tub full of Tamagotchi frogs' spawn glistening in the light of the full moon atop the Yggdrasil skyscraper.

— Ed Luker, author of *Other Life* (Broken Sleep, 2020)

Praise for *The Luna Erratum*

How do you explain yourself to yourself when you suspect that actuality – your experience of it – is provisional and full of error? You come up with your own poetics, your own tense and mode of address, which is a lunar one, and which involves speaking in crushed, frothy mouthfuls to a terrifyingly silent, unpredictable and generous friend (celestial objects, an indifferent lover, &c.).

The Luna Erratum offers no truth except in things – colours, materials, beings, dreams, schemes of language, human artefacts and locations – and their known convergences, all of which hold as much affective weight and capacity for transformation as the events that precipitated this profoundly graceful, unsettling and mesmerising book.
— **Sophie Collins, author of *Who is Mary Sue?* (Faber, 2018)**

*

A glittering universe, Maria Sledmere's first poetry collection is both lyrical and electric, both video game and watercolour. Reading these poems feels like ingesting semantic MDMA, the ectoplasm of a Victorian ghost trying to reach her lover through an unstable wifi connection. Sledmere's words ooze

The Luna Erratum

Maria Sledmere

Dostoyevsky Wannabe Originals
An Imprint of Dostoyevsky Wannabe

First Published in 2021
by Dostoyevsky Wannabe Originals
All rights reserved
© Maria Sledmere

Dostoyevsky Wannabe Originals is an imprint of
Dostoyevsky Wannabe publishing.

www.dostoyevskywannabe.com

Cover design by Douglas Pattison
Interior design by Tommy Pearson, Pomegranateditorial
Interior illustrations by Maria Sledmere

ISBN-978-1-8380156-5-7

Contents

Swerve

Solar Error

my shadow is my error—and that shadow belongs to me
[...] and now I want my errors back.
— Clarice Lispector

Lifestream

Lifestream

A particular sap is in season.
At night I am visited by fish, their tiny bodies
pulled from a book. Explaining myself to myself
    I would say *joy* is so easily hallucinated.
Couldn't load the page when I typed in *river*.
    You in your red coat, watching the deer.
Put ice cubes in the potted tree
    in your apartment
I differ in dreams from the eloquence begged;
    you don't reply. My skin is of love and salt.
Conner says you have to go through your
    feelings.
I am rolling my tarry dreams
    in the car park at the world's bright core.
I am loved by mice, rarely men
    I melt in drinks.
Close your eyes and imagine a place.
    Oven-baked, the sap was hot and thick,
needed to sit. Six years ago
we almost commented. I will learn words
    that mean the length of such quiddity.
This will be cut into coasters
    to settle a former burning, say.
Put down your glasses, software.
Mark my words—

cover us covers us.
All that I have is the currency of song:
    riverrun, rush into sutures
of future.
    The fish would leap
    and speak their research.
Little bubbles,
we look up to smile at the others,
    start to yelp.
Cars are just things in the distance,
    colour to colour, signing off.

Microdose

What premium flesh is it that meets you, moon?
I convalesce lilac all over again
Cradling Starmie in bed
And Ormelie Terrace
There are numerous ways to stream in C
    Your inbox sentiment
    Your inbox travesties
Go illuminate!
The ballad of blood is
A bad kiss, regardless
I've got the kit.

Luna I

A spiralled pool of the dark
in noonday light. I unravel
her careful snore from the screen.
Mutual susurration is loveliest
vulpecular tempo of biting down
in little nips and cuts. In private
I edit the frisky cameo of Luna
like intelligent dance music
brushing the aleatory
from a sugaring season, mews and leaves.

Love Cats

Conference pears never ripen
because capitalism stales.
Earth spins 366 times a year
but we count eleven less days;
what happens, what softens?
I took classes in revolutionary feline language
and all I got was this poem.
You can make pear butter, pickled pears,
                              lucky pear salad
or you can take bites from the sun, it's so lush
filling your mouth with fire and mourning
the last sort of leaf, passed your lips.
Misread I wanna be, wanna be pretty.
You know what they say about eleven less days.
The peak requiring of the poem is ice, no oil,
no delicate tray of blueberries (super sweet)
or back to solarity:
some illustrious zoom I find you in
a poach holism, open window
puts me to sleep, say *ow*
when she is talking to you, snowshoe.

Open World Intervention

Mincing the light in figurative intro messages
Ecco (the dolphin) and Selene (the moon)
in a sun moon cat to your sun dog it's that
blisterpack opening the shaming of sunshine is
moonshine your areola change by era
gathering moon's tears in Clock Town:
hidden water on sunlit surfaces...
Luna converses with the murder of garden bird
seasonless moonbow on Instagram
says I am Cathy
like I'm missing someone entirely

Pearlescent scrunchie around your wrist says
                              how about dinner
          & moderate signs of attention deficit

Amaryllises bloop and click so close

Tardigrades are known colloquially as 'moss
                              piglets'

All I did was jump around, explore the ocean
and croak constantly

(Born to die with the boys inside the game)

Nude

Some goldfish are meant to be stuck;
    that is the order of carnival.
Suppose we were not that, but the little
    buzz of notification, the pip
in a piece of citrus. There is too much alliteration
    in the rain to not leave this.

I do it in the morning, palms coated blue
    I go out to print on each building
like a teenager kissing lampposts,
    or Justine in *Melancholia*
who says the meatloaf tastes of ash
    and that is how I access concision
and the foliage swept back in tresses of hair
    as she opens herself to this planet.

Tender such lights you forget to see,
    the app that informs us of where we are
    when we say that we are
just standing here. The philosophical paucity
    of drawing this blue around the splash page;
beginning to say my lips stuck frost
    my infinite name in the sea.

Like the album cover,
    my room underwater, I commit this
to clove and song; which citrus is it
    that crimsons the skin,
something to believe, the clearing showers
    in a drink that calls us short?

I have been in this rain and the stars still pissing;
    the gold off another sun, its acid rising
so much to just write this
    and not lick the shape of where you fell.

Not Another Waterhouse Painting

Only that I want to see you, hope with this
cloudy grey turquoise next to it, mauve belief in
sheen, can I get away in the dark colours are too
subtle, needing more straw yellow pale Naples
and pale green I can draw in the dark but not
paint I'll go a longish walk, maybe one that
lilts / like I get vitamin D from a summer plan
she's writing in August. Today need to work on
natural colours / I guess skin peach, softness,
it's the strokes with gold or is that too corny
I would take me as far as the cemetery
needing bigger areas of colours. Take a lot
of afternoon naps. I think this needs bigger
canvases of course. Start early disorder / Make
glow & white underneath, otherwise too murky.
Rosemary you are here, we read well, it gets dark.
Like a whole patch of it & this kind of big
sweep, something ugly dramatic, say it off-
red, but the purple is lovely & especially I want
to be out & reading along in the real world.

Requisite Oil Spill Poem
After Catherine Wagner

the wind blew away the oil is a song
sirens are singing at five in the morning

dreamt Burtynsky took a photo
of my fisher-price dollhouse

a plastic pony in astrograss heaven

is happening cinematic atom
or are you not the poem that flowers
just once a year in full moon upstate Shetland

familial obligation is spilling
common gull agony aunt cloud

swoops in from miniature vehicle festival

another vegetal gap in market
trading device of the sea

scrub permafrost from my lashes

oh no is this a commodity poem, the deepest
like I give you these miniature berries...

give all time back to the tempest

Thresholds

There are points that tip.
This much oblivious.
Collect your sunlamps,
acid tears, emergency candy.
The rainforest prepares itself for release.
I had a breakdown
on the phone to my saint.
If a tree drops singles
the rainforest desiccates.
Coral flakes off its lunar spine
and starts to bleach. We live in
darkest catastrophe.
I scrape at the wax.
Bodies are still to come.
Bodies are still coming
on the line
on the notch
in your bed
I had a license to drill
and I pulled up terrible orange
and heartwood, orange
and heartwood.
Cut my peaks into rings
of celestials. Life:
push this back into the sea.

Images were clipped
to invisible blossom.
Rising, risen.
I carry pieces of forest
in the way that I speak
to make toast.
Remember what we lost
before us, glitter and twigs
of cancelled walks.
Tip, tip, tip.
There is an economy
of such excess
as to starve
and *do nature better*.

Deciduous

A shrub needs its nest.
Let's decide to salt the womb, lay precious
tiny marbled eggs. In the gallery
you browsed copious asters
in dungarees, said home is a maximalist emotion.
I was singing The Aeroplane Over the Sea
in my head; my aching brain was alive
and now it is dead. I know this sounds extreme.
Limbs of me numb and I can't go green
because of this peony. It is so much to say,
how I bled for you half of October
and fell at the gig. My roots are polished
with general sorrows, chips of moony fragrance.
How far up the canal to wander from injury
courting a swan. I love 'be there soon'
and the word *delicious*. A wee place
called Salt Horse, not by the sea. I know
this sounds extreme. I take off my clothes
in the mizzle of year, you give it away
and I sleep and I sleep. So much to say
about transport's lack. Imagine a thousand shrubs
leaving their homes in shuffle, little song of them.
My curling leaves are burning
seeds all caught in messages. I pop and crack
each one with my teeth and my tongue,

feel you inside me, at random
these verses of pollen and stars.

When is the Best Time to Announce a Floral Pregnancy?

A cube of dandelions
weep in the open field, a lily in my belly.
Do you remove a single bloom?
Mother-in-law comes by in her customary
pollen to call them weeds
which reminds you sneezingly of a childhood
                                                incident
concerning the lovely clover brought home
in bundles
like "mum I made us a lucky bouquet!"
but anything might have been trash
and crushed from suspicion
daughterly after

All the wild dandelions turn
towards different suns is a wild explanation

Had I plucked each one
the way you look at four o'clock
and turned complex ache
with only the beautiful stems
of your naming
worried a floret this all would collapse
miles ago in chamomile loneliness
everything closes to sleep

every part useful:

A catalogue of white-flowering
Japanese dandelion,
endangered Californian dandelion,
northern dandelion,
Turkish dandelion, Russian dandelion
which produces rubber,
red-seeded dandelion,
Korean dandelion, common dandelion
found in many forms, the rare
dandelion of St Kilda
will I ever go there?

Endemic to the area is also insomnia

Having assembled for you this sculpture
weeping milky latex, vomit-
a-thought, called up
lion's-tooth care or piss-a-bed yellows;
every year Americans spend millions
on lawn pesticides to have uniform lawns
of non-native grasses
an effort which uses 30% of the water supply
Here are some useful facts.

Phases

As climate changes my heart is breaking.
It broke before the heat had time to speak
by which I mean, the sky
had a hat like yours.
The word was *thinsulate*.

As climate changes my heart is breaking.
You said perhaps the right thing, wrong time
is what this is. As climate
would change, I put on my jeans.
Something has shrunk of the daze.

As climate changes my heart is breaking.
I was without need before I met
the shatterable part of the glass.
You describe yourself as furnace:
there are cycles to grief

As climate changes my heart is breaking.
We visit the forest and say
what defines us, far away;
it is a miracle, these days
that trees even bother to talk. "In reality,"

As climate changes my heart is breaking.

I have told the sparks in the branches
not to; I was noted by a hundred companies.
This wilderness is super beautiful, financial,
polished by war. As climate changes.

Mineral Garden

Love is a Kind of Echolocation

Very celery to say of your eyes
keep looking at freckles, echoes delete.
Something producing a delicate scent:
            the dulled promiscuity of lilies,
            a lip gloss spoke of puckering weekends.
At night, she scratches their ardent language.
Her lover kissed them a constellation
of vessels bursting in the multiverse.
                        It is theft to even be here.
He said he designed such stars in childhood
            as remained in his blood;
they sluiced through her, secret tattoos
of a pain extension. There was talk of them
            getting better or worse;
nevertheless, her nerves were damaged.
Something had caused the infection to flare.
                        If I read you like braille,
                        will we stay together
through every accessible future
one of them said, or did not say.
Shingle brushes the lip of a shore.
There were antivirals to take at intervals
            in which she lived her life.
They wanted to ask, will you stay.
A tabular economy of this and that.

The scent developed base notes: ferric, menstrual
beneath top layers of aster and daffodil.
Her lover stopped kissing the skin of her cheek,
        her arms, her belly, her neck.
There was only tenderness
to accompany such weather,
        soaked to the summer bones
of what she had been, yet she opened a window.
                The universe infects its kin;
                the sky is all freckles, just for her.
Later, the lingering would purple
her server of emails. At night,
it was all she could do
        to delete them one by one:
        a starry compress of the sent and unsent.

Wish Bone

Is there ever a good time to feel like this
for a person
        I take out the ice in my whisky
because Saturday.
The barbiturates are coming up fast
this year. My neighbour plants
a wish bone where her
dog died.
        I wait for 11:11
to call on your name, a habit
I can't shake since anything happened.
There is a lemonade version of sky
you say is mine
for it rises
        and like the morphine clouds
ever sleep, to be sucked
clear through a straw.
It takes off the edge.
Electrolytes I have been
in the ground
to love earth as Virgos do.
        It felt strange
to read in front of this. If you
were a perjured spirit
and not what you are

I would do better
the tipsy weeks.
            The dog was called
Smudge. Once,
he caught his cinnamon
tail on the candles.
Arrears burn close
            fur to bone.

Luna II

My body's made of crushed little stars
And I'm not doing anything
— Mitski Miyawaki

What amber is it that gels her language?
The nearest insignia will glimmer
but even the blemishes of excess
weep temporal in cinema.
She is a fugitive comma,

    not-cat, totality;

    life and death in the space of it.
She ambles a little orange for warning,
curls around the chance of a paragraph,
speaks spells for possible stardust
and loves him unconditional.

    I adore their bond

    such that I cannot translate.
Could this be midi or soft emoji,
black onyx, tourmaline, obsidian sweet
to relieve all physical harm?
It is a day like suet, pig's blood, metaphysics.
Is it safe to wear the day as she does
killing to cleanse, speaking to nausea
a wave to save this. I wonder
why Luna so often negates her stars.

What she writes of me, a quiet heat
like eating a starling.

Nutmeg Reverb

At series end, I offer credits. Whirl
not for sale, and the burning all Sagittarius

so I had known. The prairie editorial
held a woman with plaits for lashes and candy

almond limbs. I broke her off to enter the story,
chip by sugary chip. We lasted as long

as your ketamine groans could manage, leading
up the stairs, missing a kiss because of the cold

your swerve on this ice would find us
minted. Potassium assuaged

the pain, a lateral transaction
you peel my banana, very slowly

what is felt backwards about blues
is crimson read. Enzymes cluster

such edible dark, on Kelvinbridge
we speak at a suicide pace with our eyes

yet closed. Such stories not available

as the plaits unravel our internet gently.

Isn't it nice to wear better prescriptions,
to seek resolve: dusts

of luminous pollen, squandered blush,
the roots belying our warmest houses.

You are climbing a hill by the beach today
and even from here I taste your tongue,

unbrushed the lager and salt, felt
some illness correct as the hot

and hissable. We process the shine
in our common hair, take heartache

out of equations. I had assisted
in the manufacture of such plasticities

as how you held the dark in me
to the skin of a dream, just close enough

to interpret. Clipping my wings
to impossible futures, little eyries

I'd carry in prose. The night drains
what we want of morning, opalescent

and implacable light; develop the surface
to petition. Which of us enters

the course of branches and leaves
is home at all.

A short history of light

Butter light, starlight, hardly the softest light
falls thru skylight, pleasure light, telephone
light as a breeze light, pain light, the mail light
will melt on carpets & clock my light home
American light, gun light, lightest chrome
alone light, feather light, clear light, blue light
to permanent green light, gaslit sunlight
for Marlboro Light click this honeycomb
shop light, a house light, sempiternal gold
against pear light, red light, under the street
night halogen yellow, sultry light rung
as twilight back to your lover in cold
erotic blonde of good light, palest sheet
lightning inside you, really the same thing

Lawn rogue sonnet

and not to care about the rose garden
turning her magisterial sprinkler
was to occupy fragrant disregard
demand portable forest diuretic
releasing blue waters for water's sake
and the tax return of the touch-me-not
this close to formerly known as corncrake
crying in acid soil with oranges
we petal up speedy law for mowing
our wasted autumnal continuum
the billions suburbia spends on
trivial forte of what doesn't need trimming
you could plant the end to hungering grass
also abolish golf courses, worst of all

Gothic & Mundane
With a line from Anna Gurton-Wachter

This place called the Spinney
is a plateau of apple trees, pear trees, Cornelian-
cherry dogwood
                    It doesn't go anywhere!
In the movie some of us experience sunshine
or smoke each other's throats
      with a desperate thirst
the loop is an environment we all are
Lux getting laid upon astroturf
in surveillance universe
a breezy promiscuity
Happy Valentines
I am a trash apple, jazz apple
thrushy with plague and codling moth
the righteous paranoia of the English walnut
            emblossomed by sexts
                        and what does the moon do
when we get here
wintering
            the slant afternoon in suckling larvae
            having been nearly a year
                  since we touched freely
               you open the girl/boy
                     harmony of starlight
                        take all the pieces you like

& peel away
silhouette
   get to the seed

Catalytic

Body was a radical search for the engine.
A customer told me I needed a sun bed,
more boxes of chocolates. I wept
as I handed her a plate of turkey, all the
trimmings
she said were delicious, then sent them back.
    "When will this stop,
    When will I feel better?"
I was given a tiny bag of coins
to invest in some blithe aura

That was even Wednesday.
I had plans to go north, selecting clothes
    with my choking cough.
There had been complaints. Outside
    the party the sky was so gold
    it hurt to look. I knew it was wrong.
Inside, cops counted the heads
    of all bejewelled drunks. I'd love
    to call them in the morning,

Say happy birthday. A new decade
    is anyone's to piss up the wall.
Mum says, wear it when you feel
    in need of strength.

There were six points
    I pricked my thumb on each one
while licking the stamps
    I'd saved for you
a river and a change of colour.

It was already the saddest year of my life
as I recalled the story of you waking up
not knowing, then finding them safe
in the very next room. Such joy will
never happen to me.
    Like how people just
    put on movies for fun.
I could bake cakes in the middle of the night
    and watch them slump

The strange time of the owls
and how universal credit is trending on twitter.
Everyone on Instagram is having their Pokémon
chosen for them. I know exactly what I am
and this is the only thing I know.
    Why have a hill, or a breakfast.
    One time we broke the fire alarm,
that's something. Pluck the feathers
    from the owl &

Wisen your blood.
The necklace bumps against my sternum;

I had arranged strategies to cope
with the government. The further
west you go, the clearer it seems.
Makes sense to get shitfaced in mist.
She didn't know I was born
with the moon in Cancer, cute.
We felt all the petrol starting to leak.

Luna III

Everything in hand is a fractal
performing asterisk; as in smoke
you could say of fur or surface,
face in blur.

Just Transition

Big oil believe will be hit
new lyric is also tainted

With carbon capture, bruise
and storage, all serious risk

You call us onshore from
inertia, hot, you're hurting

My feelings. Global heating
to polish big algorithm

For a blush cause: mitigations
of strain emission. Sorry

We can't afford anymore.
The Scotland Act 2016

Devolved some oil and gas
licensing powers. I'm hungry

To metabolise how barrels
of oil equivalent will bury

This big debate. For general enquiries
ask greasy landlord, will you buy us

a better oven? Will you pay
for this heater, the walls are cold?

Jump to Renunciation of Poetry

hard reset : anhedonia

studding my bracelet with feminist porns

the door is storied jewellery

I suffer like an animal, meeting_saved_chat.txt

I watch the Rocky Mountains on skyline livecam

someone is quietly falling

love at high altitude, service charge

Remote pirouette of waitress

even my lungs are a tendency

leaf twinned burnish

selling her lightfast allotments

like air is 'faraway' exegesis

post-interest, the snowflakes
of coded embouchement

kill all skylarks

The Problem with Indigo

The sky is a textile conglomerate.
We bit a hole in the economic donut.
At any moment, dreaming element
or electrical storm of the movie.
All the troposphere sewn to my tongue.
Imagine if carbon came as soft serve.
One of the ghosts was a polar thought
and tasted of lyric, it split
down the middle with cream and the Earth
was inside like the stone of a peach.
Felt little buds in the cells of my blood.
Exhalations of cloudvines anywhere
I wanted to parse a more decorative energy
and I wanted to sleep forever
until everything we did was undone
as it was. Milking
computer with the moon.
Its iris became a rose in your eye
and looped back into phantosmia;
sequined the dark with notes
of underripe banana, bergamot and petrichor
curing diacritics for breakfast, varnish cache
the last of our futures scented.

How to live now, without drying the ice
afterparty, towards which our bus heaved
likeness tussocks, a snog of lost solarity
I wanted to enter with sincerity,
my hundreds and thousands
the M8 Bridge to Nowhere.

Other Side

All this talk of heartlands
and the personal, pink noise in my temples
    the spreading insomnia scroll of
    yellow and blue. Lie down awhile
as if this were closest, best; the kisses
    that mist our screens again.
I am trying to say the daylight is worth
    any hour we live by, as if still living
    by eloquent hungers, cuts to service.
We have to keep saying there is worth in this.
They are coming for us, as if we did not
open the door for those who would slam
    our cloudy reality into a tree
    they would soon chop down.
I gave you a pamphlet, you gave me a name.
I can't stop thinking of things we did:
    eating crisps at midnight, how you held
    me up in a waterfall, the dolphins
didn't mind us at all. It is a virus
we can't keep touching the winter
    inside each other. I'm sorry
    you had to keep saying it.
            Your eyes were so green

I couldn't stop saying it.
The world surrenders email yet I have sent you
the last of my sad, hard hurt.
I dreamt I was singing
a quiet, elaborate alto for love
and the cities between us cease to be.

Swerve

Improvisation is how we make no way out of
way. Improvisation is how we make nothing out
of something.
— Fred Moten

go Venus go vernal go turning go
darling by folding by buoyant kiss
— Lisa Robertson

I remember writing that love of the bent tree is
love of the swerve.
— Jackie Wang

I.

You begin with a swerve
Beginning the day as though it were over

At such moments, wisps of the Japanese maple
in late November and a pale linen
feeling that might not last
as long as you are walking uphill to meet us,
as long as you are
the last of the rest. There is a burning,
far away it once seemed greyer than reserve
                              or cirrus, some ash
falls as though it was just. Small unnameable
                              birds do not settle
and will you light a cigarette
    behind the bike shed, ten years gone
and more, to bake this into scent. Back and forth
the money goes starling, just upstream you could
                              feel the pressure
    more like truthfeel, such water as the tiniest
                              among us
feel in their plasma and is it the same as coming

                              back

how we were, life towards life

in some consequence of the plastic dish full of
                                    radiant fruit,
assorted nuclear sensation, the amnesty of another
                                    microbe
comes now to sort, incline and recoil.

When asked, you will enter the vagueness of
                                    water.
What pain is it you bring now, shining
and wild as it was to see this backwards
    happening apart from the retina,
    you peel the avatar
of one or any other sex, it is milk underneath
in the minimal literalism of the light.
The light that was mine
you patiently say, as though from a state
    the balance swings and from that beam we eat
the soft, furred peaches from their ferric tins
and sweet is the picket that seeks to leave here
clean as our uncontracted children
    drawing tomorrows as chalk
in lifelong collaboration with rain, breaking slight
    a fine-gold chain of fate
Out of sync, the leaves mourn slowly their clinamen airs
of coming solo at the moment
such reds
    as those between a phasic mist, consult

a partial language of char: no green isle, sunless
as a slow, eternal fall would be
   its distance refusing, sapless in the season now.

II.

This motion on the page is analogous to that
of the swimmer who takes pleasure in the act
that also saves her from drowning
    — Joan Retallack

In the sacrifice zone of myself, I swerve.
No tossed rituals of turmeric, the year we all
                                                   wrote
fairest of frost and I forgot to whittle my nails.
So it was deep inside you: droplet of soap,
slash invective in the stream.
Sky gets. Pink. One of three
mentions includes 'legit' and you try to speak
and the box upturns assorted sweets.
A cumulus nuclear foam of news, a chorus
soldered. What comma, unnecessarily
frail of bone and the hungering water.
If you could just learn to appreciate the trees
   like a box tick
forests are indifferent
to those who sing inside them, can you hear
the feinting coil and a lyrical split.

Getting sober again. We slay avocado
light estranged. Optative

verse for the monstrous among us, one
of our kin must burn. I caught you kissing
the end of the sentence, becoming pith.

It meant big things like possession
and the mirage of Fire Island was only
pink light on the opposite window
from which you saw a solar figure.
It glyphs for the literal measure.
These static missives; I was in the daylight,
undecided. How did you not get hungry.
I was an Alice, an Icarus.
I watched you clawing green meat
from the skin of a memory, slipping
just so in a similar bed
would I unlock the all in reverse?
Your breath was oceans in my ear
and so—

III.

The numbers, such as they were
could not correspond to a season.
Autocorrect the liminal with your gelatine
print, portfolio sales. In such cloud
as this anaphylactic blackness, you are stung
so many times as to wither the government.
    Fuck the autumn weather, plenitude of stems
and lyric apples; fuck everything in the menagerie
                                        now
you can't get up, thorax, stray violin and veering
west to south like air. I wanted a sheer
definition of *lyre*; liar, leer
at the starting scene. Play-press
to collect this, parcel abundance
stuck couriers. I love
you like milk loves milk
before it is sold
a sour war, a platitude.

Dearest appraisal of day in the seam.
Swerve is a move of consciousness
accordant to blue
or nuclear red, internal burn
even prior to cloud; even that
particular snow, so pink it would make

a nurse blush to tend the skin
so burnt by it. Pray-less
the village were moving silkier into themselves
in masses of communal water; a drunk man
comes to repair the starling
not far from my father's lodge.

Will you ever have sex again, I ask the crow
who visits my lovely English oak
and spreads its loving black on the green
and swivels around in the wetness
of all that black, shiniest feathers
stirring to melt in the liquid
breeze I see with. The emphasis of moon
has been. Sweet imperilled self again,
we have no use for your atoms
we gather up your bitten dreams.
The crow is cautious.
The crow is a pronoun, don't say
the wind in the grass is changing course;
the crow is anachronism.

This is the picture of the lake that was taken.
This is the hungriest daisy, lackadaisical
I am become flower; I swerve in the breeze
which is only lyric.

Summoning out of syntax.
Close our pretty face at night.
My iPhone detects a faceless ethics
as though I had Levinas on speed dial already
sufficient to ever corrupt the line.
    Baby's cry dot em pee three,
the beneficial empathy, duly served.
Have I said what I have had to say of a swerve
when the car pulled in and almost killed me
quick as a kiss,
    redeliver your life.

Touchstone shimmer, eight-bit lyric
carry your nerve in the kissing
be less of the bloom you become
as lace. I tie up loose ends
for you in the hold, enter gravitational
we become apposition. She lets herself
towards becoming less: gives away
her clothes, sparkling dolls, her cancelled glitter.
They enslave polyethylene terephthalate
in our fish, this literal, it is likely
the glitter will teem in our seas.
I relinquish my hold in eucalyptus cellulose
enhancing 'natural selection'
astride our brazen shine. It is promiscuity,
mutating in quick, November air
as though contact itself were ambient only

where you realise the also in the am
I are; them are us too
and a late perishing, a curl of protein.

Anecdote is super effective.
Goodbye first love, goodbye, goodbye
I tidy my shoes. You split a lace
and count the elegant swans by the lake
we only painted. Tiny glitter in your eye
was almost blinding. I let my fingers graze
the rocks and leaves, pleading feedback:
Yohuna, Eudaemonia.
The cars tipped overnight
    a glass of wine
I see the salt-dried oils before me
Firefox reveals all spent earth in churlish pastels,
as if Camille had not drawn up the plans
and held her own. Desire exists
in twisted red, susurrations between glass panels
and these exquisite remains of a tree.
    Life is good to know,
a deciduous shot that flares and falls
in corpus of writing, I forget my aphoristic lust
in message body, crying on her kitchen floor—
five years have passed, five elisions of summary
in which light at eight is a miracle paragraph
we live by the calyx of online status,

a singular ovular green
beside the smallest, familiar face.

IV.

Striations of body produced by irreducible math.
There is a fidelity that moves in stereo, separates
the one from oneness, declines
sweet as a breaching fruit
and starts to bleed. I called you
because I could not attend the march, was clipped
of human mono. Had only instead a tonal cry
all up Pollokshaws Road, all night
in the unseasonable, September heat. Falling
after forest, you're just not.
    I want to add
one holiday to the voice that would hear me.
Multiplication blues again.
You're sick on the bus, making stops
of the voice that is beautiful and dumb
like a Tesco wine. I like that
    the whale is a wraith
of unknown scream, the one we studied.
    I cried alone in the Hidden Garden
while children rang rings
of poesy around me
palest white
late summer, long shadows
and I was just blood
    in the belly of the bluest wail.

Water is memory's ingredient: carry it,
carry it lilting to the air.
    What language is it that sexuates the nameless
with skin in the line of a wound
you could trim like grammar.
Little organ rainstorm, comb
the mist from my hair. I like that polarity
compresses the light. In tender waters
addressing trace.
Something so long of a voice
you could not cut its sex.
    Imperfection there is
you will see, more basic sauces
fill the sea. The lifestream almost on
I saw it, parts of your life
blown glass backwards
greatest, greatest
and everything I tried to think
or fuck up the cherry pie of your life
at the start of a week, who'd have me.
Fred says, 'choice is in the water'[1]

and there is lead in the water
                        I thicken
on a screen of black midi
where somebody makes cursorial swerves

---

1 Moten, *The Feel Trio* (2014)

84

across the glass.
   Is it beauty to say this,
tornado emoji for serial conjecture.
Click on my face to solve the dream.
Yeah there's a document of air,
blood in the water
avatar truance.
   All tresses of mist
in afterglow, a skylar continuum
of the seen—
   Be here with me.
If I can't change, I can listen.

Soft, clickable infinite.
A cut in the long division, lengthening ruin.
You make rumours
of truthfeel, tannin, drips of light.
Valerian thresholds of sentient life
where I pluck a rose to measure
apocalypse please.
   Cinnamon roll, remove from your freezer
the requisite basic space of glass.
Something borrowed, the particle spiral
of fresh conjecture.
   Adulterate theorem fluids,
make me into a movie.
Everyone will know

in the future what happens.
Everyone will kiss the moon
with abandon particular to ancestry
and silent creases of the sea.

Inevitable thimbles of feeling
collectible

Solar Error

Foam Theory
After Colin Herd

Dear unbreakable day
I have been trying to get through
with my small hammer, sixteen hours of loss.
It has been two weeks. The universe is made
                              of foams
and if we knew that, we would know
this happening is only so much as
what survived the last burst, ocean's surface
sprawled in space. I could
hit out a pattern of time and not get done,
raising my brows to the visible.
   Did you mean to make this happen
   or was it the ache?
In the dream I had a contract to kiss
the first person who gifts me a bubble glass
refusing to break. My sister lacked shoes;
we walked earthquakes to find a love
that would clasp us happy.
Where are your bubbles.
No tool survives the foam
but a decorative attitude to life itself
               keeps circling, circling.
Each bubble will process the world's info
                    thrice in shimmer.

Consider the scale of it.
You spread the bubbles across my belly,
watch them pop; I have seen you
doing this in adverts, movies.
   Sentiment proliferates.
Do you ever belong to the day?
Approaching your softness
at the very phase,
would you come back,
kiss me quantum?
   The bubble is full
   with universe.
      It is full of the kissing.
      I could blow you a dream.

With Love & Solarity
For Katy

Careless, braiding the fur of a pear
I look for nourishment in water

as though it were other, something
to be peeled and left beautiful

in a state of undress. Have you seen
a lime without skin? All of my

friends have chemical burns from
working in bars, the juice reacts

with what sparse light we acquire
this north. A rind on the floor

is lunar grammar. You could just
cut into wax another thought,

softening feasts of it. The hour has
a casual tenacity I'd link to strata;

all prior hours stacked freesia
the work of exchange, which happens

in wires and clouds. I forget to use
soap; the line feels briny. Ocean

becoming a perfect sphere, angelic
with avatars, loosening new

celebrity halos. I say anthropic
to alight from the email, shining

with several extinctions: matters
of plundered velvet, kelp beds

we slept in eons before. I want
to roll around the Earth again;

I fall off my calorific plateau.
This specific fruit lacks seed,

it stresses a surface. Nothing
grows back like the violet hurt

of forgetting a paleo exchange
in awkward phosphenes.

What if the pear bled tender
and tried to scream; would it slit

without juice, a radium lyric?

I could make playlists of this;

I could collect the lovely
adverts in chorus. Nevertheless

we slant towards sun. It is only
the origin story of a special excess

which cools without section.
Everything falls online, with enzymes

until what ceases is more than a rain.
The door kinda opened in the air

again, I drew bright circles
in the sky to find it.

Flirtation Device

What's the hottest and coldest
place you've ever paid a visit
I don't talk about Mars though perhaps I should
make a list of incorrigible holiday destinations
        remembering layering sun cream on
                      peanut butter
and turning lapels into kissing sensations
all your dream of having better jacket
lined with petals, silks and other prophylactics
only to take (it) off for me, so we stand
in the freezing together — 1, 2, 3
I am sucking the ocean dry and enjoying its salt
in my pink gums, I am authentically soaked
reproduction: on the other side of earth
                you spread this very slowly
so as to suffer the atrocity of snowfall
one or more times a day, sliding under
when I am brushing my teeth
you shovel it thick back into the river
                  that same water
bottled on eBay, snowflaking and lovemade
in the handcrafted atmosphere of general arousal
I have felt marsquakes in sleep
the ocean goes through me as I through thee
have swallowed a song with my t-shirt gone

and my lilypad breasts and frog heart yearning
to eat between sips of expensive h2o
you sob back into red snow thrust
against us with high berry confidence falling
wherever you've been within a greenhouse
as glass has shattered in Spain
from the weight, the earnest weight
say Mars was once much wetter and warmer
I have never been to Iceland, alas
my indigo rose tomatoes, my dead stars
the naturefuck is a hatefuck?

Reconnaissance

Oliver says
give drone a go.
He was referring to metal.
I guess it was
morning. It didn't feel good.
I wanted to lie
in the grassless space
where a tiger should be.
My reality was a rusted
corrosion of focus;
the droning metallurgy
of air raids. It was neither
here nor there.
They served evil cakes
in the kind of casing
turtles choke on.
A thing
like that. Taste
of history, sugar;
mycological nostalgia
not predatory lyric.
It goes
on and on
and on.
The sea,

the sand,
a line of bass.

Tiger, tiger

The sheep here are fake and belong to what
forsaken windsock is in no time
to edit the series of instinct,
more or less modern
than modernist specialities:
                              cinders, juice-
                              Joyce, brand of coke
we huffed our way to the reading,
you bought me a crook for £9.99
stately and gave me a coat, it was shearling
I stood on top of the hill and read new poetry
of Blakean mainstream, a laminate lamb
in what is called anglophone practice
    this sick roseate heart
the crowd were my grasses singing
each of them fake chewed by vocal fry Texel
& Blue-Faced Leicester
on earth as it is in churches
the light is sweet it is stained with
                              avant-garde caramel
I wore white linen as in *Capital*
I was hypothetically twice as valuable.

Hot Rat Prince

Looting third-dimensional world
saying the sun is a cowboy

I have given so much *these days*
unnameable rows of orchids

oily of aura swallowing the rat
to say only I want you, been so long

since a lariat beat would snare
in the trailer, how stallions

never really get to fuck
Ane says I am the star-faced

emoji, sublimating my outro
for something only the rodents know

in mathematical confusion meme
Chopin was almost normal girl

squealing the rim with finger for entrance
only the clarity now is a mote

Embarrassment Hack

The embarrassment of sunshine

Is a burn on my arm

Embarrassing to admit

Like you are a portable math

And kimchi noodles

This one cool trick for making 'dinner'

The embarrassment of Aloe is her sister Vera

The embarrassment of alarm

Is the act of 'going off'

I guess you like that, don't you

The embarrassment of spice

Is all things nice and mellow

Sorry, boys!

The most embarrassing emoji

Is goji berry cheeks on yellow

Kinds of smiling rhyme

The embarrassment of my childhood

Was another brass instrument

Time I fell asleep during the principal's speech

And dropped my trombone

Or was it Glenn Gould

The embarrassment of water

Is being conceived in Niagara Falls

The embarrassment of soreness

Is only not having enough

Sass on the bus

Same as a blush is

The embarrassment of Capri-Sun

When I can't get the straw through and

Message you, how do I eat these noodles

In sunburst hour of sadness

Lady and the tramp myself

Back to embarrassment

At the end of the line is all

The embassy listening to our calls

As if I would write this.

Generation Why

A child wears a hoodie whose slogan is
life is better with wifi

Our parents are shopping

in the tinderbox city, footpaths closed

and blue, blue / I hold it together
because I have to

walk for miles, my eyelashes blister

in dulcimer cinders, Joni sings of a lurch,
a fatherless love

& sawtooth notes are anyone's:
entropic of concrete

lying down. Our signals

glisten just so, we all want to take off

on a bike lane, raising health
there is space to sweat, to part.

I brandish mascara

kissing your name,

consider the hipsters.

My phone is a beautiful place

attuned to the flammable sea.

I want to throw it forever.

You don't call, or can't. Stopped by a match,

I cry my eyes out by the Clyde

with this case, so much of it not.

Lunacide

Lunacide

Experts warn rats 'bigger than sheep'
will roam our planet / and I a vile girl
knew this already, purpled of bone and fur
    she told me I had to get better
but treatment is typically characterised by relapse
and the why of the rat is pathogenesis, oppression
beyond your cherry-red shoes, your past & future
                          smoky music
is only I love the heat in the last
incredible sunlight for miles. Rats love the heat
and I was a rat. I want to extend my tail to you.

Dichromatic, gasoline
reading colours in blur
we enter a lemonade garden of trashes
    the colour-blind flowers
become glasses of chardonnay, pearly ombré
of tomorrow's snowstorm...

    Gaining weight at the end of the world

Rats are our future ancestors.
We die off the edge of language, arriving thrice
In recovery still ashen in the cryosphere of
                    chronic hypoglycaemia

a sex empties out, drunk and generous
To eat as often or necessary as desired.

A lunacide.

A love story.

In one study, only female rats were used
to examine practices of restrictive dieting.

Insufflate ecological niche.

You wipe the screen of your laptop clean.

Sucking on chilblains

I dream a convex stomach of special eternity.

Rats are really beautiful

Kissing with a brokenness they felt in my ribs

Ascension Day of the Scream.
Apocalypse is so damn moreish.

Could Earth destroy the moon?

I have a lot to learn. Do you:

a) read this ad libitum
b) take zinc supplement
c) restrict

       I'm fat as a rat
         fat as the cat
       that ate my rat

Baby, it's only gravity

Trampled by other luminous families
My bodily informant, becoming vermin
              she is with fleas <3

The white-hot rat you set in glass polis
to swim below in milkweed swamp
streaming violence, streaming violence...
I curl around you for hours, vile hours
             in orbital constant...
I want to ascend...

       out to graze with my allies and the corner
          of this page is trampled for life

   if I was a moth, I was a mother

(splash of flesh and delete this forever)
Osteoporosis, liar's glacé, Laura Palmer's cocaine
Reynaud's, my shivering nervosa
texting exit the lodge
for last trash animal of the anthropocene.

My Rodent Sisters

> Then a strange imperative wells [...] either stop
> writing, or write like a rat...
> — Deleuze and Guattari

(as) drunk, (also mad, poor, rank, weak, etc.) as a rat catch like a rat in a trap, to do (also pull) a rat, to feel rat shit, to get a rat, to give (a person) rats, to go to rat shit, to have rats in one's garret, to like a rat up a drainpipe (also drain, rope, pump) like rats leaving a sinking ship not to give a rat's ass (also arse) rat-arsed rat bait rat-bat rat-bean rat-bird rat bite fever rat-borne rat-brained rat cage rat-catching rat charmer rat cheese rat-clam rat-coloured rat-deserted rat-eaten rat-eyed rat-faced rat-fat rat firm ratfish rat flea rat fuck rat fur rat-gnawn rat-grey rat-hare rat haunt rat horde rat house rat hunt rat-hunting rat in a trap (also cage, corner, etc.), a rat-infested rat-inhabited rat kangaroo rat killer rat-kind rat king rat labour rat-land rat leather rat-like rat-mole rat office rat pie rat pill rat pit rat plague rat poison rat-poor rat preserve rat printing office rat-proof rat-ridden rat-riddled rat rule rats and mice rat's ass rat season rat shit rat-shrewd rat skin rat snake rat's nest rat-souled rat-swift rat-taker rat terrier rat-tight rat-toothed rat warren to smell the rats, get your rat out

It's this light within rat

Shall we leave the gig and get on a night bus
for coastal miscreants, in mosh pit
watching the waves do loneliness
   I want to be
      rockpool.
We have these beers

and feel abandoned, cracked open, crawling
   melodic, almost
talking in a bad freud:

My body, my body
is somebody's cosmic encore
did it have signature like time-
              play logic
        near threatened, vulnerable, endangered
         sporadic cousin
         or general glacier?

Six million years of people having thought
is a firmament, but
they also love shoving each other
   not like coal
in the small dark philosophy
oceans of no applause.

If I were more of a morbid unicorn

Deep litany for shelter
and messages, viral frolic
we come by auroras in thrall of the mall
in spiralling nylon
mom gave me fishtails of lace
we listen for horse neighs and narwhals
at the harpsichord store
you could make them cry as a kid
and I could just cry
dolorous acid quantity
now, would you like that
squinting my eyes of rays
with mortal lines
say what you will
say of the garbage & flowers.

Upping Your Online Blues
For Conner Milliken, on his birthday

Dolly says, if you want the rainbow
way I see it, you gotta put up with the rain

In a bad little house on the prairie
blossom grows wild to read this sideways

The blossom = thesis
& Sickness < botany

another compulsory meeting...............
circle the arboretum............

How did they forget we were in this to dream?

It's noon and I'm watching Miley play Jolene
where the grass is long and endless green,
lucky horseshoe necklace

I want the auburn. Hey, the loss
was in the green and song.

She appears on the subway
   smaller than leaf, she is a literacy.
      Imagine not knowing how many songs
      you had already written, thousands
               resolve
          in the tears we forget

feeling to know, press this into cassette, breath
on yellow legal pad ~ scrawl melopoeia of not-
happiness
yes

        I said, "that's the Botox"

Who populates the suburbs
with other coyotes. Cliché
versions of Drapers drop litter
on municipal lawns for hours.

  Heartache / the fault
    in our plastic stars,
  rhinestone eyes...
Emmylou Harris, twentieth century
              'mother nature'
Someone better give me my cigarettes

Gouge harvest moon from my rat eyes.
          Say a word like 'highway', over and over...
                    Another intervention
          in timelines light and lying. Lauren Berlant:
                    '"We" live our lives as works
                    of formal beauty, if not art.'

          Felt Taurean
          and pushed through the bullshit so fast

could I be a pop star to know
another bluegrass afternoon
I can't face the fact | I'm not important to you

Someone better give me my cigarettes
                    nicotine steady as rain, neck this.
Little office on campus, you pay me a visit
with such business as the sunflowers wilt in
the applejack password
saloon boys are all sooo bad
                    We'll never be rich like them
                    We see an altered nautical twilight

Huge in our hair, a spray of plagiarised lectures
shotting each date of the tour
of your lounge bibliography

as distance is social
Copy/paste destiny
before we wake, Linked in
pale elegia for employment

Why not search yourself into a wage??

And I wrote this for annual progress
at the laundromat, endless review of tuille
and pastel aporia
you look good smoking on Zoom
and I'm here for you, crying
at the end of comedy again

It's only a perfect day in the eighties.
Hope is a crush you punish
to be dangerous, I had to strip
the sky of denim
and start on sensuous volta...
Light of a clear blue paragraph,
fringing language; everything's wrongly

dumbest, sweet suede, dealing me
poppy seeds and whisky
We just have to dream
for the fuck that we give

it all refracts
the union
in email rain

      Post-quarantine, I'll have the script,
      copy and themes, bring tins

Here for you in a google doc, in the salon
among lavender velour

         I'm begging of management

  please don't take what we have to live.

Luna IV

Local businesses close and are closing
as Luna says a very good thing,
the way you say it was good
of a coffee or egg,
perhaps vat of milk. My faith in taxing
the infinite, like how ill-lighted the place
is now and you crush into mutual sugar
the hours
spent anyway waiting, as if
consumers would fix this solvent economy
of varnish and trash, our flesh is so
imitation, rainfall
flipped and wet.
Something is boiling
the logic of property.
Do you put this sherbet
on the soft and future profit;
do you open the room
where a stranger is literally billowing orange
and something smells very nice
but you can't be certain.

Covivid

She was not in San Francisco having a shower
this close to exorbitant fever soap

Stepping from an episode
of *The Twilight Zone*

Blood in decorative thermostat
getting in line for asylum breakfasts

Take photo of unreachable shine sprite
to be infinite (objectivism)

Rest in aperture of the sunlit kin
I had no fetish for lovelessness

This rash on my arms a google alert
like the onset of breath from god

The beautiful boy in the street
is opening the door of a car

Vulpine Precinct

Skulking around on refusal plateau and city not being the city. Poem wrote
because encountered other poem in the street
about a month ago was it, other poem in the street
remember the street. Other poem was staring at the alley cat; foxes do that.
It's like how young my brother looked in the Facebook memory
and the hula hoops in the garden, nobody doing anything with them.
You go out, general lamplight, being this hungry.
Things I have to jump through only to, no, is the poem a carnivore.
Jump through or towards, elongate, nobody expects to see me here.
Dead of night again. Bushy little clouds.
Night is relative and foxes listening, elongation...
You go into the pub and into the poem. This is a politics.
You go into the pub and the poem, it's howling. Words for busy shift:
shafted, hammered, pumped, flooded, fuck.

Words for customers are words for plumbing, and then fuck at the end.
Is a plateau always level and with what. Words
for asphalt; stand in them. Saw poem in the street again
was it yesterday maybe. Poem looking sly
with tail curled around me. It goes like

Ring-a-round the rosie was a plague poem,
pail of water, a wandering robin lonely
the boys are singing the boys are singing
after the ashes, berries and flowers
colours dying eventually...............

I'm delivered a website that claims 'nursery rhymes, in general
are the worst things anyone has contributed to the world.
They almost always contain dark themes such as handicapped-animal mutations,
infanticide and even a possible murder-suicide.' Poem says
what rhymes with kiss

a backup device with your name on it, foxes are listening
and bunny bit the dust as usual...
another three hula hoops around the sun, that's corona
O animal aura of plasma
a black hoop, a blue hoop catches the wage. We sign out half an hour late,
supervise flowers and ashes... Catches the rabbit.
We are punished for this, being prey to poems.
As if the foxes bring us back to city. Electric, we're leaving now.

Totalities

If someone disappears,
we will write their name
in the waves again. Thank you
for paying my entry, hanging my coat.

The Fox and the Otter

Means water, where you had been in your holt
with the bevvy, so much for rivers
of state-funded vodka and blues.
Don't pussyfoot the night for answers
since a river will skelp you dry; just plunge there
and trust the current. It is so sad
to think of the years we won't have our lives.
From now on, the stream is crying
for the way you sat with her, curled just so
sunlight treasures you same.
She waits at the door I draw in my dreams
with her tail thus crooked to sickles of moon.
Beneath these roots, learning to hunt
the careless creatures in their shells,
my jaw is gone like a heart. Most species
will their water to log in the land;
they try to speak or fuck one another.
A countersign required to evolve.
If we applied the same time, our hunger
opening wild, our forest of loss
we hold in crisis
because not to know is to live now
without SUVs, surveillance or pain.
This means water
because not to know is to live as if

the days were poached by earlier methods
and you brush my russet coat, and you love
backwards like the owls do.
Accessible land still blisters the flow
and we run, and we run into orange
to stop this. I prowl
the city for lack of a home
and you sent me the photo of sunset,
six am, months before scrambling
was only the kisses, soft insomnia
of novocaine mammal I am.
After the sex of it, my teeming eyes
fill with Andromeda visions, swirls of paisley
wasting days within me
so warm, salt-pelted; the morning
with lint on nylon, a limited palette.
This is the improvised theory of living
tooth to leaf, tongue to fur
as angelic principle
the water after all
I love you and I want you to win.

Acknowledgements

Cover design is by Douglas Pattison.

Illustrations are by Maria Sledmere.

'Lifestream' was published in *PAIN* issue 4, with thanks to Vala Thorodds and Luke Allan. Extracts from *Swerve* were published in *Prototype 2* and 'When is the Best Time to Announce a Floral Pregnancy' was published in *Prototype 3*, with thanks to Jess Chandler. 'A short history of light' was published in *The Stinging Fly* issue 45, with thanks to Cal Doyle. 'Just Transition' was commissioned by nicky melville in collaboration with Interview Room 11's Four Letter Word project. 'Tiger, tiger' was published in *PERIODICALS* issue 1, from Death of Workers While Building Skyscrapers, with thanks to Lucy Wilkinson. 'Generation Why' is named after a song from the Weyes Blood album, *Front Row Seat to Earth*. 'My Rodent Sisters' is sourced from the *OED*. 'Upping Your Online Blues' quotes from Lauren Berlant's *Cruel Optimism* (Duke University Press, 2011). 'It's this light within rat' is named after a line by Alice Notley, and its first line is taken from graffiti that appeared on the boarded up, post-fire O2 ABC venue in Glasgow (RIP), in winter 2019.

Epigraphs are gleaned from Gilles Deleuze and Félix Guattari, *A Thousand Plateaus: Capitalism and Schizophrenia*, trans. by Brian Massumi (Continuum, 1987), Clarice Lispector, *A*

Breath of Life, trans. by Johnny Lorenz (Penguin, 2014), Mitski, *Puberty 2* (Dead Oceans, 2016), Fred Moten, *All That Beauty* (Letter Machine Editions, 2019), Joan Retallack, *The Poethical Wager* (University of California Press, 2003), Lisa Robertson, *3 Summers* (Coach House Books, 2016) and Jackie Wang, 'YOU MAKE ME FEEL #2', *Entropy Mag* (2014).

Immense gratitude to Colin Herd, Katy Lewis Hood and Rhian Williams for reading drafts of this manuscript, to Sophie Collins, Nadia de Vries and Ed Luker for the kind words, to Tommy Pearson at Pomegranate Editorial and to Richard Brammer and Vikki Brown for constant indie comradeship.

This book is for Luna.

*

About the author

Maria Sledmere is an artist, occasional music journalist and poet based in Glasgow. She is editor-in-chief at SPAM Press and member of A+E Collective. Her pamphlets include *nature sounds without nature sounds* (Sad Press, 2019), *Rainbow Arcadia* (Face Press, 2019), *infra•structure* – with Katy Lewis Hood (Broken Sleep Books, 2020), *Chlorophyllia* (OrangeApple Press, 2020), *neutral milky halo* (Guillemot Press, 2020), *Sonnets for Hooch*, with Mau Baiocco and Kyle Lovell (Fathomsun, 2021), *varnish//cache* (If a Leaf Falls, 2021), *Polychromatics* (Legitimate Snack, 2021) and *Soft Friction* — with Kirsty Dunlop (Mermaid Motel, 2021). With Rhian Williams she co-edited *the weird folds: everyday poems from the anthropocene* (Dostoyevsky Wannabe, 2020) and her poems were included in *Makar/Unmakar* (Tapsalteerie, 2019), an anthology of contemporary poets in Scotland, edited by Calum Rodger. Her poem 'Ariosos for Lavish Matter' was highly commended in the 2020 Forward Prize, and an epistolary work with Katy Lewis Hood, Tangents, was longlisted for the 2021 Ivan Juritz Prize. A collaborative exhibition, *The Palace of Humming Trees* (2021), was recently presented at Glasgow's French Street Studios, with artist Jack O'Flynn and curator Katie O'Grady. *The Luna Erratum* is her first collection.